1.   The Russian winter

2.   The tailor's song

Hebrew

2

3. Cradle Song

Polish

4. Folk Dance

Swedish

5. The theft

Hebrew

6.   Varshavjanka March

Russian

7.   Black cherries
(duet)

Russian

8. Ländler

F. Schubert (1797-1828)
(Austrian)

9. The soldier's signal

Bulgarian, arr. V. Milanova

10. My beautiful Balkans

Bulgarian

11. Folk Song

Ukrainian

12. Dance from Swabia

L. Mozart (1719-1787)
(Austrian)

13.   Auf der Alm

German

14.   Wind, tell my sweetheart
(Gipsy song)

Hungarian

15.   Swanee River

Stephen Foster (1826-1864)
(American)

16.   Cielito Lindo

Mexican

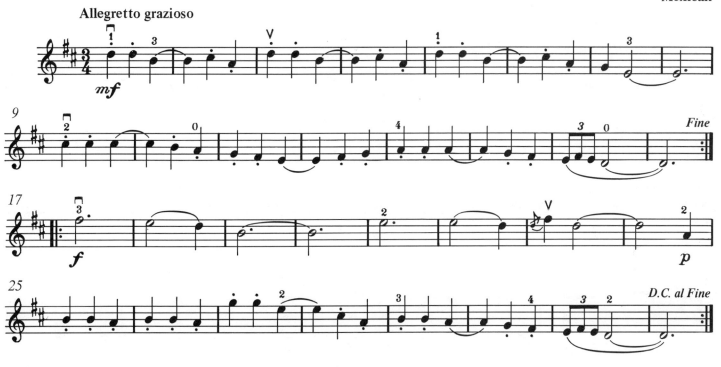

17.   Rhodopi
(Mountain song)

Bulgarian

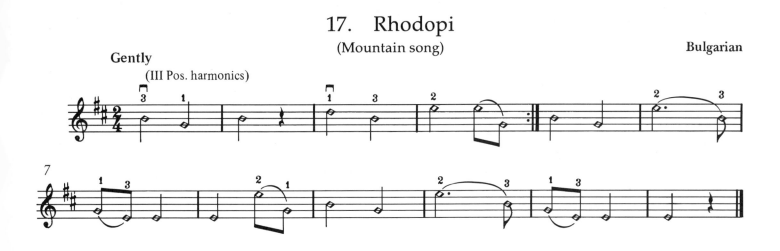

18.   Harvest time

Bulgarian

19. The little goat

Bulgarian

20. German Dance

L. van Beethoven (1770-1827)
(German)

21. The Cuckoo

A. Arensky (1861-1906)
(Russian)

22. Sleep, my child

Hebrew

23.   Folk Song

Swedish

24.   Blow the wind southerly

English

* Stretch 1st finger back without changing position.

25.   At the well

Austrian

26.   Cossack Dance

Polish

27.   The Deil amang the tailors

(The Devil among the cornfields)

Scottish

28.   The Mallow Fling

British

29.   The bashful bachelor

Irish

30. Pizzicato Mazurka

Polish

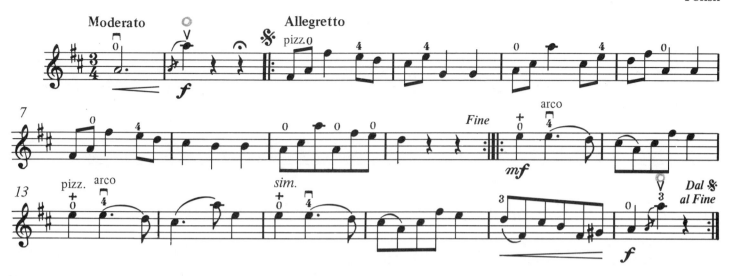

31. The bush in bloom

Irish

32. A letter to mother

Hebrew

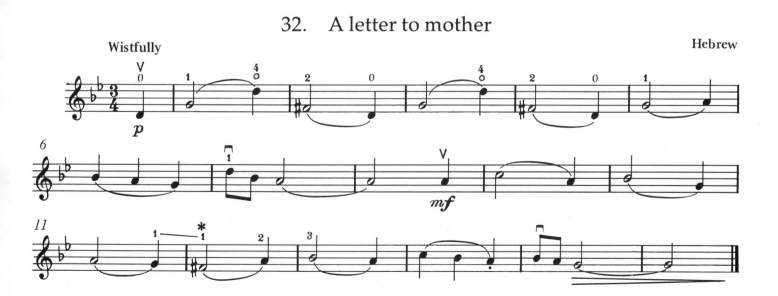

* Stretch 1ˢᵗ finger back, without changing position.

33.   Far away, near the river
(duet)

Russian

34.   The gipsy bear dances

Bulgarian

* Stretch 1st finger back without changing position.

35. Back to Sorrento

Italian

36. Juanito

Chilean

37. Sinaian Hora

Romanian

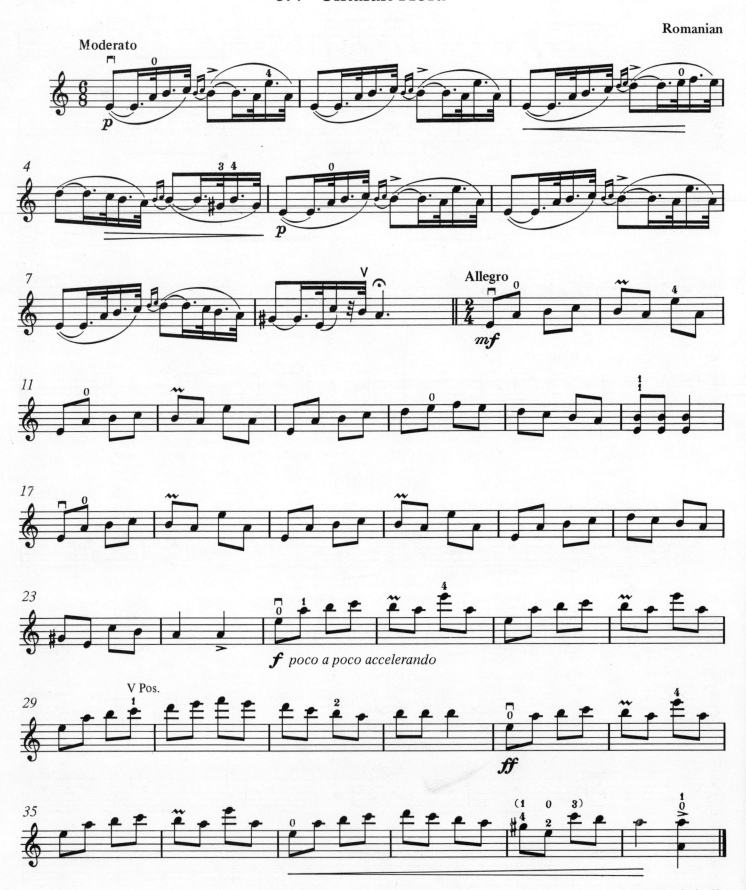

Reproduced and printed by
Halstan & Co. Ltd., Amersham, Bucks., England